Najc

LIFE IN THE FAST LANE

INSIDE A HIGH-SPEED TRAIN

COLLIN MACARTHUR

Cavendish Square
New York

Published in 2015 by Cavendish Square Publishing, LLC
243 5th Avenue, Suite 136, New York, NY 10016

Website: cavendishsq.com

This publication represents the opinions and views of the author based on his or her personal experience, knowledge, and research. The information in this book serves as a general guide only. The author and publisher have used their best efforts in preparing this book and disclaim liability rising directly or indirectly from the use and application of this book.

CPSIA Compliance Information: Batch #WS14CSQ

All websites were available and accurate when this book was sent to press.

Library of Congress Cataloging-in-Publication Data
MacArthur, Collin.
Inside a high-speed train / by Collin MacArthur.
p. cm. — (Life in the fast lane)
Includes index.
ISBN 978-1-62713-043-1 (hardcover) ISBN 978-1-62713-045-5 (ebook)
1. High speed trains — Juvenile literature. I. Title.
TF148.C44 2015
385—d23

Editorial Director: Dean Miller
Art Director: Jeffrey Talbot
Production Manager: Jennifer Ryder-Talbot
Production Editor: David McNamara

Packaged for Cavendish Square Publishing, LLC by BlueAppleWorks Inc.
Managing Editor: Melissa McClellan
Designer: Tibor Choleva
Photo Research: Joshua Avramson, Jane Reid
Copy Editor: Kristine Thornley

Printed in the United States of America

CONTENTS

High-speed trains are the fastest of all trains.

High-speed trains make our high-speed lives easier by getting us to places faster. There are high-speed trains all over the world. For some trips, high-speed trains are quicker than cars and airplanes—and you don't have to wait in a long line to go through airport security!

High-speed trains are the latest and most exciting trains in transportation history.

Horses pulling wagons along cast-iron rails.

TRAINS THROUGH THE YEARS

Railroads have always tried to increase the speed of their trains and reduce the journey times since trains were first introduced.

Earliest Railways

During the Roman Empire, people used wagonways, an early form of railway. The Romans cut grooves into bumpy stone paths. They built carts with wheels that fit into the grooves. People or animals pulled the carts. The grooved **tracks** smoothly guided the carts along the road.

Wooden tracks were used in mines in Europe during the 1500s. Wagon wheels were placed on the wooden **rails**. Horses or people pulled or pushed the wagons along the rails to and from the mines. Wooden rails were replaced with cast-iron rails. Cast-iron rails, however, were easily damaged. Modern rails are made of steel.

Early Uses of Trains

During the 1800s, different communities were growing and developing that were far apart from each other. People in rural areas needed supplies such as food, coal, and lumber. The invention of the train made delivering supplies much easier.

The first trains were powered by steam engines. These engines had the power to pull more weight for much longer distances than horses could, and in a shorter amount of time. Trains could carry thousands of pounds of supplies. This power and carrying capacity made trains the best way to transport supplies over long distances.

The **locomotive** is the part of the train that powers its movement. The locomotive is named after the type of engine it has.

The Power of the Steam Engine

In 1804, English inventor Richard Trevithick built the first full-size steam train. His steam train looked like a huge barrel sitting on wheels. The barrel held water and a coal fire burned beneath the barrel. When the water boiled into steam, the high-pressure steam

Steam-powered locomotives produced clouds of steam and smoke.

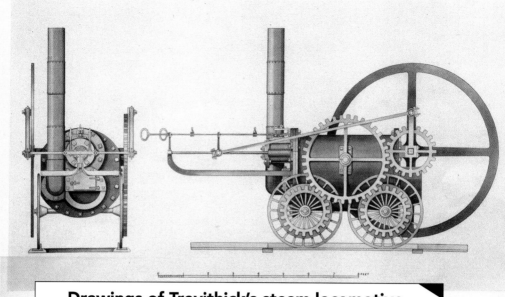

Drawings of Trevithick's steam locomotive.

moved a piston back and forth. A bar connected the piston to the wheels. As the piston moved, the wheels turned. In February 1804, Trevithick's **steam locomotive** made the first steam-powered train railway journey in Merthyr Tydfil in South Wales.

Trevithick's first steam locomotive, however, was too heavy for the cast-iron rails in use at that time. But he did inspire other people to design and build better steam trains.

The first successful steam trains were built for use at mines. They were able to haul several coal wagons hitched to a steam locomotive. A group of coal miners also could ride. These trains were not large. The locomotive and carts used in mining were narrow so that they could fit into narrow tunnels. Steam railway lines expanded throughout Britain. They were first used to transport goods between cities. Soon people wanted to use the railway to travel between cities too.

Before the mid-1800s, the central part of the United States was a vast wilderness. Railroad workers laid tracks through this land. The trains that ran on these tracks had many stops along their routes. Towns sprang up along the railroad lines wherever the train stopped.

These small towns soon grew into cities. Trains helped in the development of cities by bringing people and supplies to the rural parts of the United States.

FAST FACTS

Before steam trains, the fastest form of transportation was the stagecoach. Stagecoaches could carry only a few people at a time. Stagecoaches were pulled by horses and traveled at a speed of about 7 mph (11 km/h).

In 1848, a steam train reached a record 60 mph (97 km/h) for the first time.

By the 1850s, steam locomotives were used throughout the world. Steam trains carried supplies and people to different parts of countries and continents.

In 1869, the first U.S. transcontinental railway was built. Tracks laid from the east were joined with tracks laid from the west. This railway made it possible to travel from one coast to another. The distance from New York to San Francisco is more than 3,000 miles (4,828 km). A trip this far would take six months by wagon train. But steam trains made the same trip in six weeks!

Electric and Diesel Trains

Steam locomotives did have some problems. The steam engines made a lot of noise and smoke while operating. The engines also needed a constant supply of coal and water to operate. Train builders tried to find new sources of power. By the end of the 1800s, inventors were working with electricity to power trains. **Electric trains** replaced steam trains in the United States in the 1930s.

A diesel train called the Zephyr arriving at the station at East Dubuque, Illinois.

Electric trains were faster, cleaner, quieter, and easier to run than steam trains. They could carry more cargo and more passengers. Today, electric trains are used in many parts of the world. Electric trains are powered by electricity that runs to the train from an overhead wire or a **third rail** on the track. The electricity is made by an electric power plant. Diesel-electric trains were invented in the early 1900s. They are electric locomotives, but the electricity is generated by an onboard engine. This engine runs on diesel fuel rather than coal

Modern diesel trains can pull very heavy loads.

INSIDE A HIGH-SPEED TRAIN

and water like steam trains. These first **diesel trains** were faster than the electric trains of the time. They were also more powerful than steam trains. In 1936, a diesel train called the Zephyr set a long-distance speed record of 83.3 mph (134 km/h) from Chicago, Illinois, to Denver, Colorado.

Today, diesel trains are less costly to run than electric trains. Diesel trains are still used in areas where it is too expensive to use electric trains.

Introduction of High-Speed Trains

Traditional trains in use today travel not much faster than trains did more than 100 years ago. Most normal passenger trains travel less than 100 mph (161 km/h). High-speed trains average around 150–155 mph (241–250 km/h). Many go even faster.

FAST FACTS

Steam trains still are used in parts of Asia. Some other countries are also bringing them back because the cost of diesel fuel is so high. They are also used on historical tours in the United States and other parts of the world.

The latest models of high-speed trains look like machines from science fiction movies.

2 HIGH-SPEED TRAIN DESIGN

Many countries now use high-speed trains, and each nation brings its own flair and style to train designs. But trains aren't changed just to look better; they must also solve specific challenges. No one wants noisy trains, so each new design should be quieter while increasing the engine's power. These trains also must haul heavier and heavier loads, but be able to accomplish this task on the existing rail lines. The trains should be faster, but remain safe to use. A train that **derails**, or jumps off the tracks, can cause serious problems. Finally, traveling by train must be cost-effective, so building new trains must not be too expensive.

Working with the Landscape

One of the greatest challenges for train travel is the land's topography, or shape. Early trains could not go up steep hills.

Tunnels and bridges allow trains to go through hills and mountains.

INSIDE A HIGH-SPEED TRAIN

Tracks were laid around hilly land and mountains. This caused the routes to be longer than necessary. To make routes shorter, tunnels were blasted through hills and mountains. Blasting and tunneling were very expensive. The early steam trains also filled tunnels with smoke fumes as they passed through them. This smoke was harmful to passengers and livestock. The invention of high-speed trains allowed railroads to be built over the natural land. Powerful high-speed trains can easily climb steep land. Blasting through hills became unnecessary. Electric- and diesel-powered trains do not create dangerous smoke when they go through tunnels.

High-Speed Train Tracks

High-speed trains run on their own special tracks. These dedicated high-speed tracks are made to handle the faster speed of trains. Tight curves are dangerous for trains traveling at high speeds. The specialized tracks have long curves that are angled (like a banked curve on a racetrack). This design keeps high-speed trains from tipping over while going around curves.

Dedicated tracks have special rails, too. The rails are welded together end to end so that there are no spaces between their connections, making them smooth and even. This improves the ride by reducing vibrations and bumps along the rails. These rails also don't have the "clickety-clack" sound of regular rails.

Older tracks used by regular trains can be modified for high-speed train use. When high-speed trains use these older tracks, they must run at slower speeds. Older tracks have tighter curves. Some high-speed trains have been designed to tilt when they ride on modified tracks. This allows the train to go faster than normal and still provide a comfortable, safe ride.

Train Design

There are many different styles of high-speed trains, but there are some things that all high-speed train designs have in common. A high-speed train needs to be fast, safe, easy to clean and repair, and quiet. Designers think about every need when they design the outside, inside, and bottom of high-speed trains.

**Dedicated tracks for high-speed trains
are angled along curves.**

The sleek design of high-speed locomotives offers little resistance to the air.

Outside the Train

The high-speed locomotive has a front shaped like the nose on a jet aircraft. This design helps the train move through the air more easily than ordinary trains. Air pushes against all moving objects, causing resistance. Resistance makes moving objects run slower. This jet-like shape allows a high-speed train to move through the air with little resistance. With less resistance, a train can go faster with less engine power. When less power is used, operating costs are lower.

Trains moving against air also make noise. This noise can be heard by passengers and by people who live near the train lines. The smoother the shape of the train, the less noise it makes as it moves through air. Designers limit the amount of sharp edges over the entire outside of a high-speed train.

Inside the Train

Trains traveling more than 100 mph (161 km/h) create air, or pressure, waves.

These waves can cause pain in the human eardrum—they have enough power to shatter glass. To solve this problem, high-speed train cabins are airtight. The cabin pressure is controlled from the inside like an airplane. This way, any harmful pressure waves or loud noises don't affect the passengers. Designers also try to soundproof the cabins, making the ride as quiet as possible.

Early train **engineers** watched for signals along the tracks about track problems ahead. These signals were colored flags posted by the side of the tracks. As train speeds increased, spotting the warning flags got harder. When the drivers did spot the flags, the trains went by too fast for them to see and react to the signals in time.

Today, high-speed train engineers ride in cabs designed with a wide view of the upcoming track area. Huge colored lights hang above the tracks along all routes. Engineers can see these lights from more than a mile away. If a light warns of a problem ahead, engineers have time to stop the train. Some high-speed trains now go too fast to even see these signals. These trains are computerized and receive signal

The inside of high-speed trains is similar to that of airplane passenger areas.

information electronically from the rails. All trains are equipped with computer systems that guide and monitor conditions of the ride. The computer also allows controllers at the station to stop the train if there is an emergency.

The Bottom of the Train

The wheels are an important part of the high-speed train system. A high-speed train has both driving wheels and support wheels. Driving wheels are located in the front of the train and are turned by engine power. Support wheels carry the train's

Wheels and rails for high-speed trains are designed for high speeds.

weight. They allow the rest of the train, which is being pulled by the engine, to move. Wheels are held in structures called bogies. Bogies connect two or more pairs of wheels to the train car.

As the train moves and the wheels turn on the rails, this motion causes the train to vibrate, and this vibrating increases at high speeds. The more that trains run on rails, with heavier loads and faster speeds, the more rails wear down. To lessen this wear, designers are looking to build lighter trains to decrease the weight bearing down on the rails.

Eurostar trains are very popular in Europe.

3 HIGH-SPEED TRAINS AT WORK

High-speed trains are usually for passengers and not freight. Most freight service is done by electric or diesel-powered trains, but some high-speed trains do move freight. More and more countries are building high-speed train systems to meet passenger needs both within their own nation and for those travelling to neighboring countries as well. High-speed trains are becoming a popular choice for daily commuters. Major high-speed train systems and their locations include:

- **Shinkansen**—Japan
- **TGV**—France
- **Eurostar**—London to Paris or Brussels
- **ICE**—Germany
- **CRH**—China
- **KTX**—South Korea

Thousands of people in these countries travel using high-speed trains every day.

Japan's Bullet Train

Many people believe the Shinkansen in Japan to be the first true high-speed train. In the 1950s, Japan wanted a fast and convenient form of mass transit to relieve traffic congestion. The Shinkansen was its answer. The word *Shinkansen* means new super express in Japanese, but the trains became known as "bullet trains" because of their shape and speed. The bullet train started services in 1964. Today, it is the most heavily traveled high-speed rail route in the world. Shinkansen has never ceased

Shinkansen Hayabusa high-speed train at the train station in Tokyo, Japan.

to evolve. New models of Shinkansen trains use more advanced technologies, including automatically changing speed, high-tech brakes, and more comfortable passenger seats. The E5 series Shinkansen model, called *Hayabusa*, (Japanese for falcon), travels the Tohoku Shinkansen Line between Tokyo and Shin-Aomori. Travelling at speeds of 199 mph (320 km/h), it is the fastest train service in Japan. The hope for the future of Shinkansen is even higher speeds. Some foreign visitors fly all the way to Japan just to enjoy a ride on Shinkansen.

TGV high-speed train speeding through the French countryside.

France's TGV Service

Train à Grande Vitesse (TGV) was the first high-speed rail service to reach more than 155 mph (250 km/h). In 1981, the first line was opened between Paris and Lyon in France. TGV has had many historic speed records, reaching a record 357 mph (574 km/h) in 2007. There are three major lines leading out from Paris. Passengers can travel to Belgium, the Netherlands, Germany, and Britain.

What is special about the TGV line is the aerodynamic styling of the nose and that the cars are semipermanently attached to each other. The trains are run with a locomotive on each end, so they are symmetric and reversible. Countries such as Spain, South Korea, and the United States have adopted the technology of TGV trains.

TGV trains are so successful and popular—air routes have been reduced or deleted on some lines—that it has been called "the train that saved French railways."

Travelling Europe with Eurostar

The Eurostar high-speed line runs directly from England to France and Belgium. It connects the three countries' capital cities of London, Paris, and Brussels. In 2007, the High Speed 1 (HS1) line opened, the first high-speed rail line in England. Now the Eurostar can travel at speeds of 186 mph (300 km/h) in both England and France. Passengers can board the train in London and be in Paris in just over two hours.

The Eurostar system uses 27 TGV-designed trains. The trains have 18 coaches and 2 locomotives. Each train can carry 750 passengers per trip. In August 2009, Eurostar carried its 100 millionth passenger.

A tunnel beneath the English Channel was made specifically for the Eurostar service to link England and France. The tunnel is called the Channel Tunnel, or **Chunnel**. The Chunnel is 31 miles (50 km) long, and 23 of them are underwater! The tunnel has three tubes, each with a rail track. Two tracks are for the trains going in each direction, and the third is a service tunnel. Within the Chunnel, trains travel at a reduced speed of 100 mph (160 km/h) for safety reasons.

Germany's Intercity-Express

The Intercity-Express (ICE) trains began service in Germany in 1991. Since then, they have expanded to the Netherlands, Austria, Switzerland, and Denmark. The ICE trains are very popular. In 2009, more than 77 million passengers rode on ICE trains.

There are five different train types on the ICE lines. Some of the ICE trains have windows at either end where passengers can see into the driver's cabin and out to the tracks. Most of the trains run on older, modified tracks. In 1999, they introduced tilting

Entrance to the French side of the Channel Tunnel.

trains that could travel at 30 percent higher speeds on curves. Some of the trains run on dedicated high-speed tracks at speeds up to 200 mph (320 km/h).

The ICE trains plan to expand to London in the future. There are many changes they have to make to their trains first to make them safe to use in the Channel Tunnel.

CRH380A model is presently the second fastest regularly operating train in the world.

China Railway High-Speed

China has the largest high-speed rail network. China Railway High-Speed (CRH) began service in April 2007. The original trains run on existing lines that were upgraded to handle higher speeds. The CRH trains are among the fastest high-speed trains in the world. The CRH380A model is designed to run at speeds of 236 mph (380 km/h) on the newly built Chinese high-speed lines. It was put into regular service along the Wuhan-Guangzhou high-speed railway in 2010. CRH380A trains travel from Beijing to Shanghai providing daily service to thousands of passengers.

The Korea Train Express (KTX)

The Korea Train express (KTX) is South Korea's high-speed train operated by Korail. KTX trains connect Seoul Station to Busan in the south. The KTX design is based on the French TGV trains. KTX trains came into service in 2004. They can reach speeds of 217 mph (350 km/h), although speeds are limited to 186 mph (300 km/h) for safety reasons. KTX trains can accelerate really fast; it only takes 6 minutes and 8 seconds to reach 186 mph (300 km/h). Around 160,000 people use KTX trains every day. A new line is under construction to serve the 2018 Winter Olympics in PyeongChang.

FAST FACTS

The United States uses high-speed trains. The **Acela Express** began operation in 2000. The train links Washington, D.C. with Boston and New York City. It does not use a dedicated high-speed rail line, so it only reaches a maximum speed of 149 mph (240 km/h). It is still faster than regular rail. Passengers can travel between Washington and New York City in under three hours!

Maglev train traveling at 268 mph (431 km/h) through suburban Shanghai in China.

4 FUTURE OF HIGH-SPEED TRAINS

High-speed train travel is increasing worldwide. Many countries have plans to increase their high-speed rail lines.

There are many benefits to high-speed trains. For trips between 160–560 miles (250–900 km), high-speed trains are quicker than cars and airplanes. When you add up the travel time to the airport and the time to check in and go through airport security, the door-to-door travel time is much quicker for many trips by high-speed train. Higher prices of fuel for jet planes also make high-speed train travel a better option for passengers. Most high-speed trains use electricity for power, so they can be powered by renewable energy resources. The Eurostar trains make up to 80% less carbon dioxide emissions than flying. Finally, high-speed trains can be more comfortable and give passengers more space than cramped airplanes.

Levitating Trains

Maglev is a shortened combined word for magnetic levitation. The Maglev uses magnetic power to **levitate**, or float, the train over a rail called a guideway. The levitating height is about 1 inch (2 cm). Magnets are placed in the ground and on the train. The ground and train magnets push against each other, which forces the train to rise up and move forward into motion.

The first commercial Maglev began service in 2004 in Shanghai, China. It is a prototype, or model, and goes just 19 miles (30 km). The trip takes just over seven minutes.

Because it can travel at speeds of more than 300 mph (483 km/h), the Maglev is closing the speed gap between ground and air travel. Airplanes fly at speeds of 600 mph (965 km/h) and are best for long trips. However, high-speed trains will be used more and more for short trips. The Maglev's speed means that train travel time will be cut in half from what it is now. Imagine—London to Paris in just over an hour without leaving the ground. Maglev technology soon may make that possible.

MAGLEVS OF THE FUTURE

Japan plans to build a Maglev line to connect the cities of Tokyo, Nagoya, and Osaka. The first segment is expected to open by 2027. The trains are being tested in central Japan and reached a speed of 311 mph (501 km/h) in fall 2013. Japan also hopes the U.S. will buy its Maglev technology for a line between New York City and Washington, D.C.

Vacuum Trains

Engineers are working on plans for the fastest high-speed trains yet. They are called vacuum tube trains. There are various designs but they all have one principle in common—to pump all of the air out of a sealed tunnel and then shoot a train through it. These high-speed trains could theoretically hit speeds of up to 4,000 mph (6,437 km/h), making them much faster than air travel. New tunnelling technologies need to be explored to make it all possible. However, if these super-fast trains were to become a reality, the trip between Beijing and New York would take less than 2 hours!

WORDS TO KNOW

Acela Express: a U.S. high-speed train line connecting Washington, D.C., and New York City and Boston

Chunnel: the tunnel beneath the English Channel, used by Eurostar trains between England and France

CRH: the high-speed train system of China

dedicated track: a track designed and used for a specific purpose

derail: leave the tracks accidentally

diesel train: a locomotive with an engine that runs on diesel fuel

electric train: a locomotive with an engine that runs on electricity

engineer: a person who operates a train

Eurostar: a high-speed train system in Europe linking England to France and Belgium

ICE (Intercity-Express): the high-speed train system of Germany

KTX (The Korea Train Express): the high-speed train system of South Korea

levitate: to float above the ground

locomotive: the part of the train that provides the power for moving

Maglev: a train that uses magnetic levitation as a power source

rail: a bar that forms a track for the wheels of a train

Shinkansen: the Japanese high-speed train line

steam locomotive: a locomotive with an engine that runs on steam power

TGV (Train à Grande Vitesse): the high-speed train line of France that serves several countries

third rail: an additional line in a track that supplies electricity to the train

tracks: iron or steel bars or rails on which wheels are placed

FURTHER READING

Books

The Best Book of Trains
Richard Balkwill
New York, NY
Kingfisher
2008

Train
John Coiley
New York, NY
DK Eyewitness Books
2009

Trains
Amy Shields
Margate, FL
National Geographic Readers
2012

Websites

Amtrak
www.amtrak.com
Amtrack provides intercity passenger train service in the United States.

Eurostar
www.eurostar.com
Eurostar is a high-speed railway service connecting London with Paris and Brussels.

Shanghai Maglev Train
www.smtdc.com/en/
Shanghai Maglev Train is a magnetic levitation train, or maglev line, that operates in Shanghai, China.

RESOURCES

Organizations

National Association of Railroad
Passengers (NARP)
505 Capitol Court NE, Suite 300
Washington, D.C. 20002-7706
www.narprail.org

Railway & Locomotive
Historical Society, Inc.
www.rlhs.org
Founded in 1921, is the oldest organization
in North America devoted to railroad history

20th Century Railroad Club
P.O. Box 247
Arlington Heights, IL 60006
www.20thCentury.org

U.S. High Speed Rail Association
10 G Street NE, Suite 710
Washington, D.C. 20002
www.ushsr.com

INDEX

Page numbers in purple are images.

INDEX

About the Author

Collin MacArthur is a former automotive engineer with a master's degree in mechanical engineering. Today, Collin works as a freelance automotive interest writer. He lives in Florida with his wife, son, and dog.